10 BEST Digital Paintings
by Larry Murk

I0467780

Preface

I, Larry Murk, graduated from Stanford University in 1987 with a bachelors degree in computer science. In 2000 I suffered an accident that caused a spinal cord injury leaving me a quadriplegic. Luckily I can still control my arms enough to operate a computer reasonably. I have always been interested in art and being confined to a wheelchair has led me to explore the world of digital image creation. My image editor of choice is named GIMP. GIMP is very similar to Photoshop except that it is FREE so I highly recommend everyone try it out. Visit the ClassicsGold Youtube channel to view videos of how each painting was created. I hope you enjoy sharing these images as much as I enjoyed creating them.

Siberian Tiger

The Siberian Tiger embodies awesome power combined with elegant beauty.

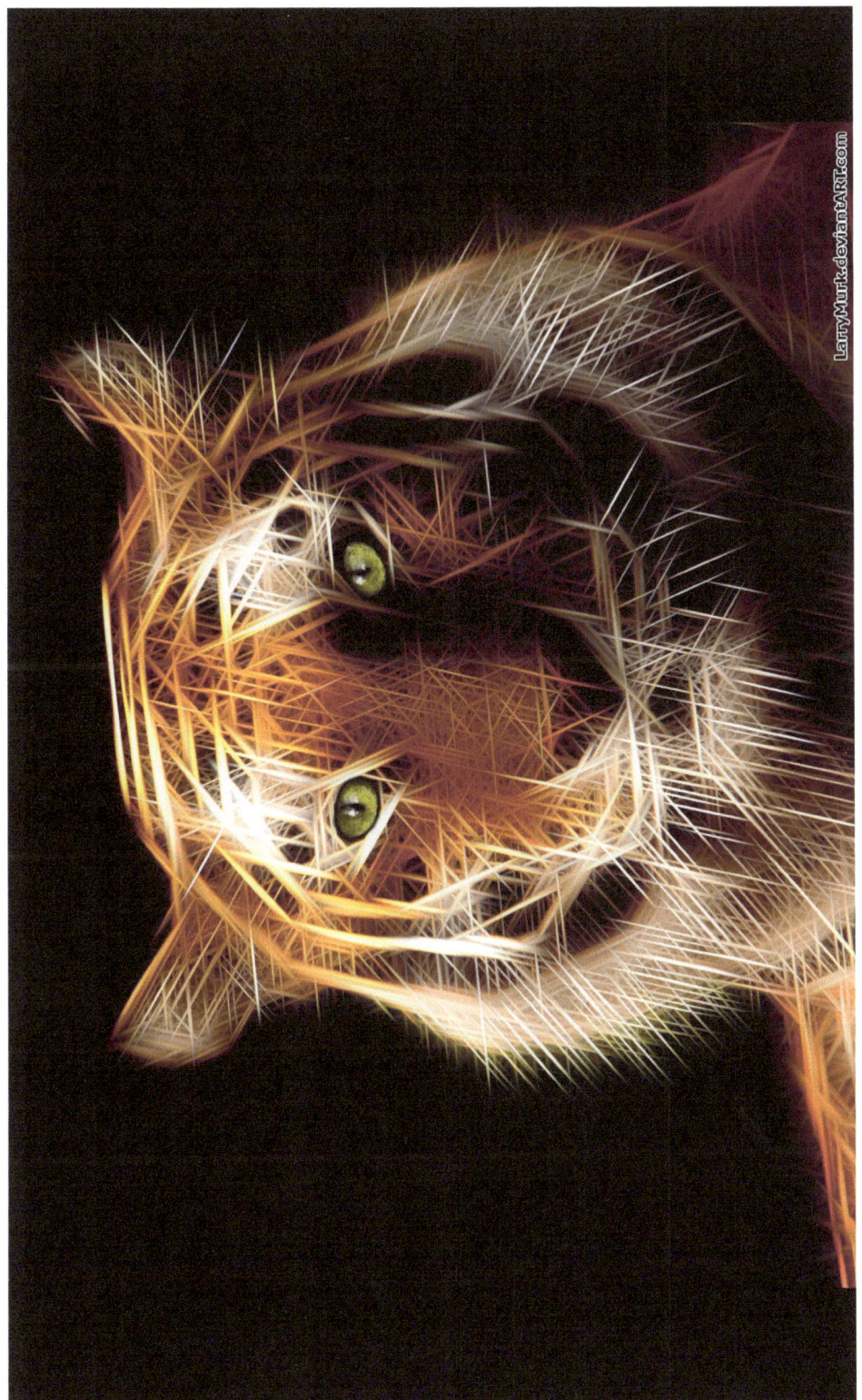

Egyptian Pyramids and Purple Planet

A huge purple ringed planet and several different colored planets lie in the background of three towering Egyptian Pyramids.

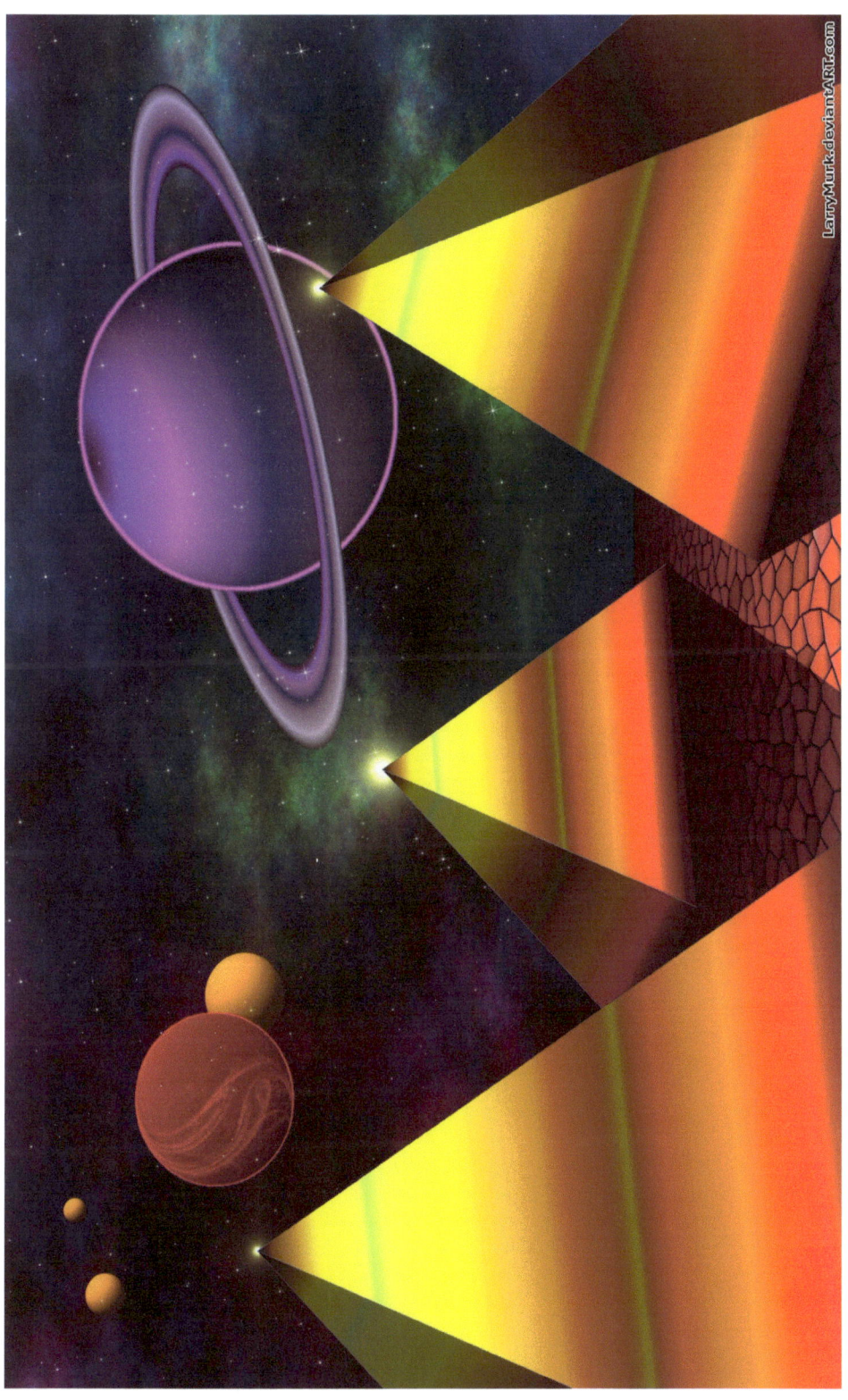

Fractal Wonderland

Enter a fractal wonderland where every step you delve into its infinite space opens new undiscovered detail.

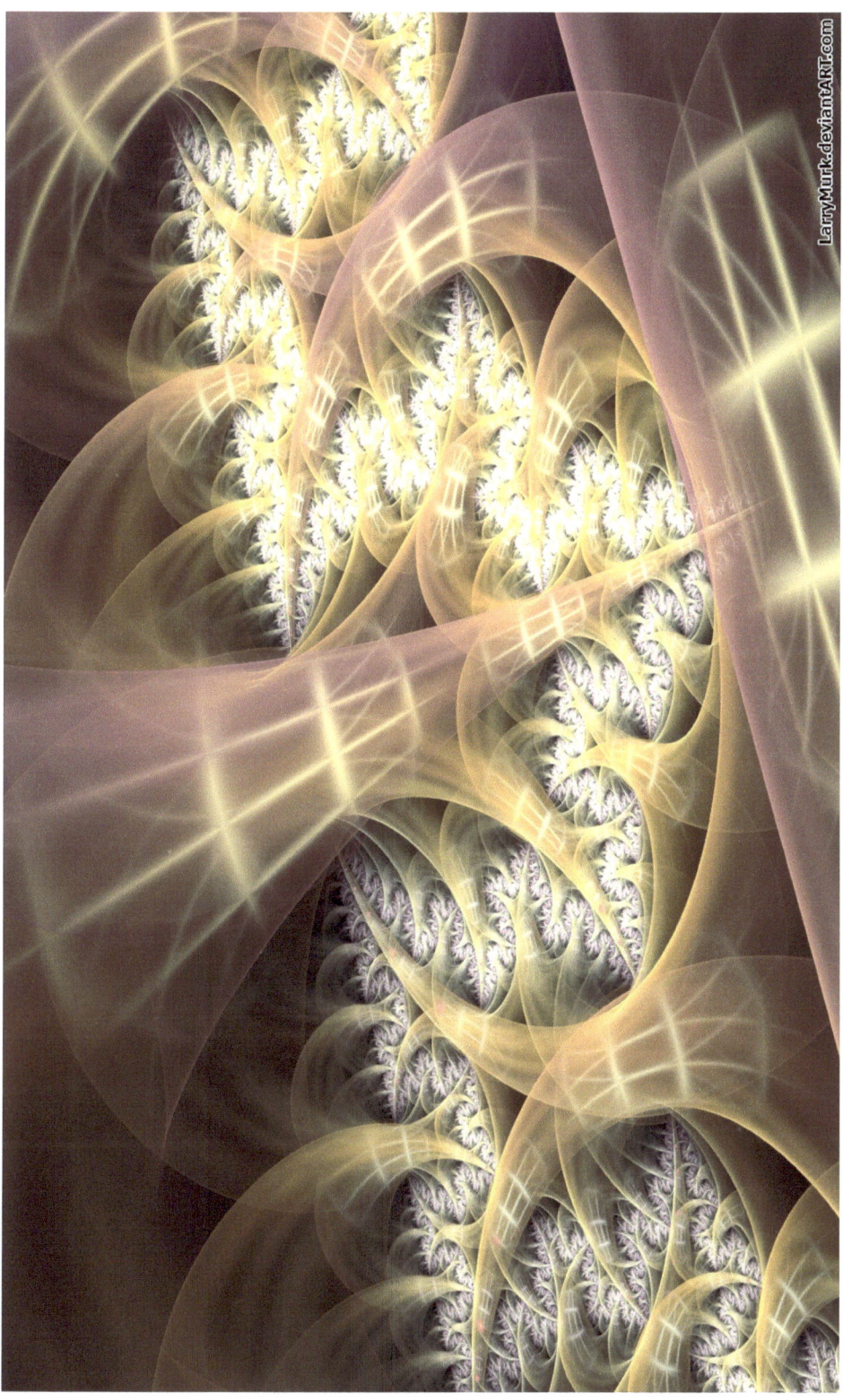

Moon and Star over Lake

The full moon rests lazily in the heavenly evening sky casting its light gently across the shimmering lake.

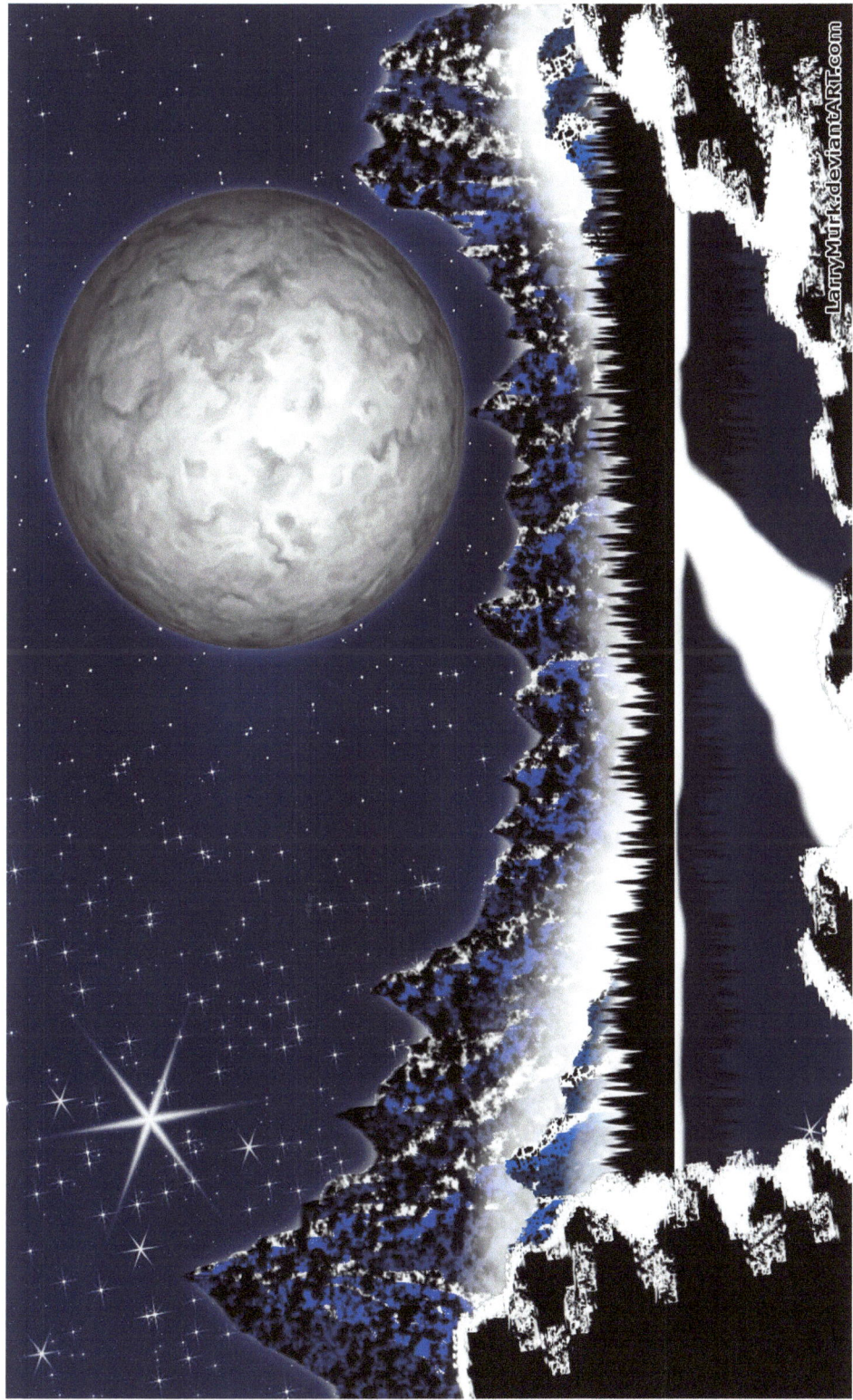

Alien Red Dome with Golden Aura

What significance does this alien red dome radiating a golden aura possess?

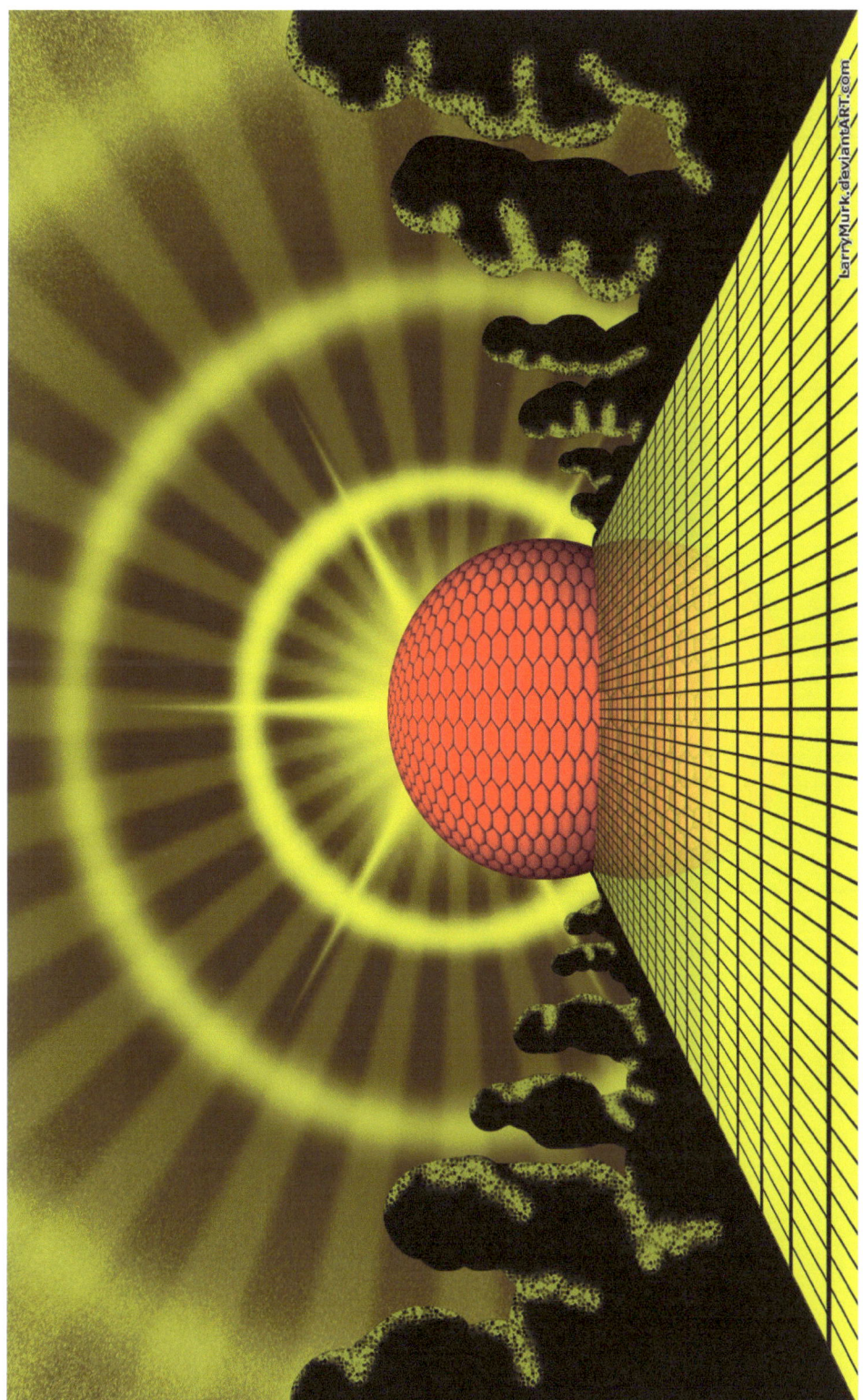

Rainbow Bridges Sun and Rain

If you follow the rainbow you just might turn rainy days into sunny skies.

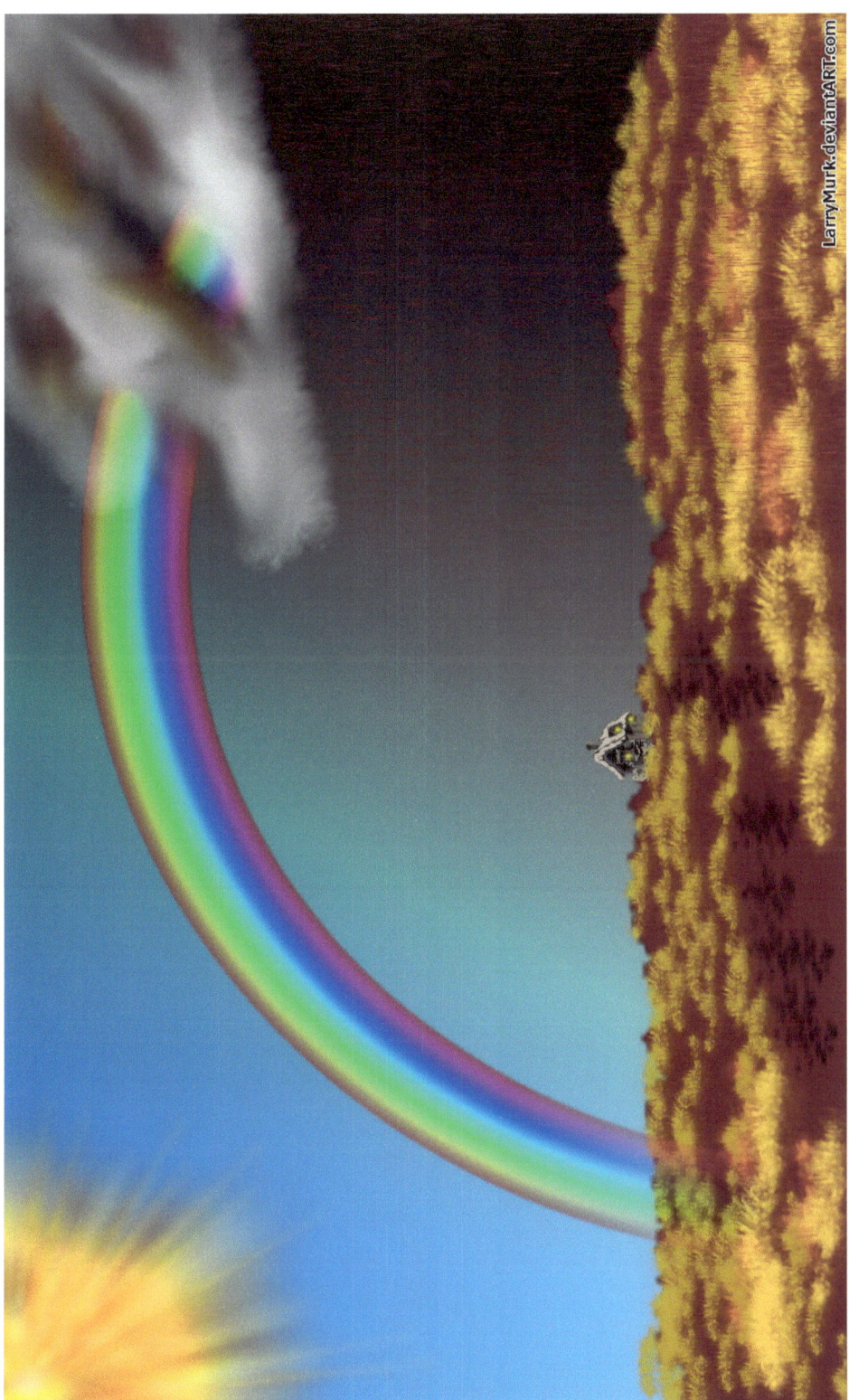

Mountains Reflect on Icy Lake

An ice covered lake reflects the faces of majestic mountains looming above.

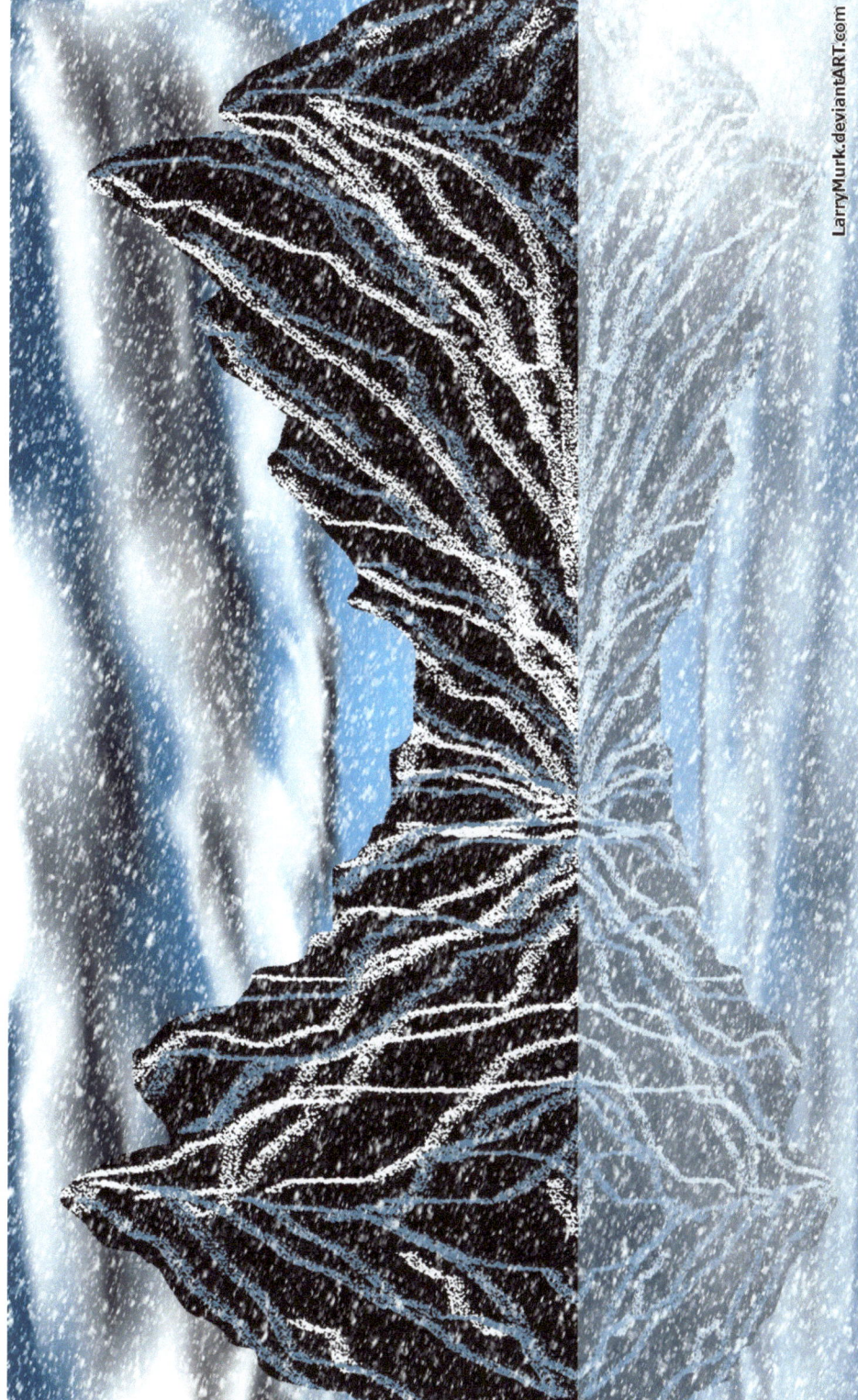

Cave and Colorful Planets

Looking out from a cave you marvel at the fabulous sky littered with bright stars and colorful planets of blue, green and purple.

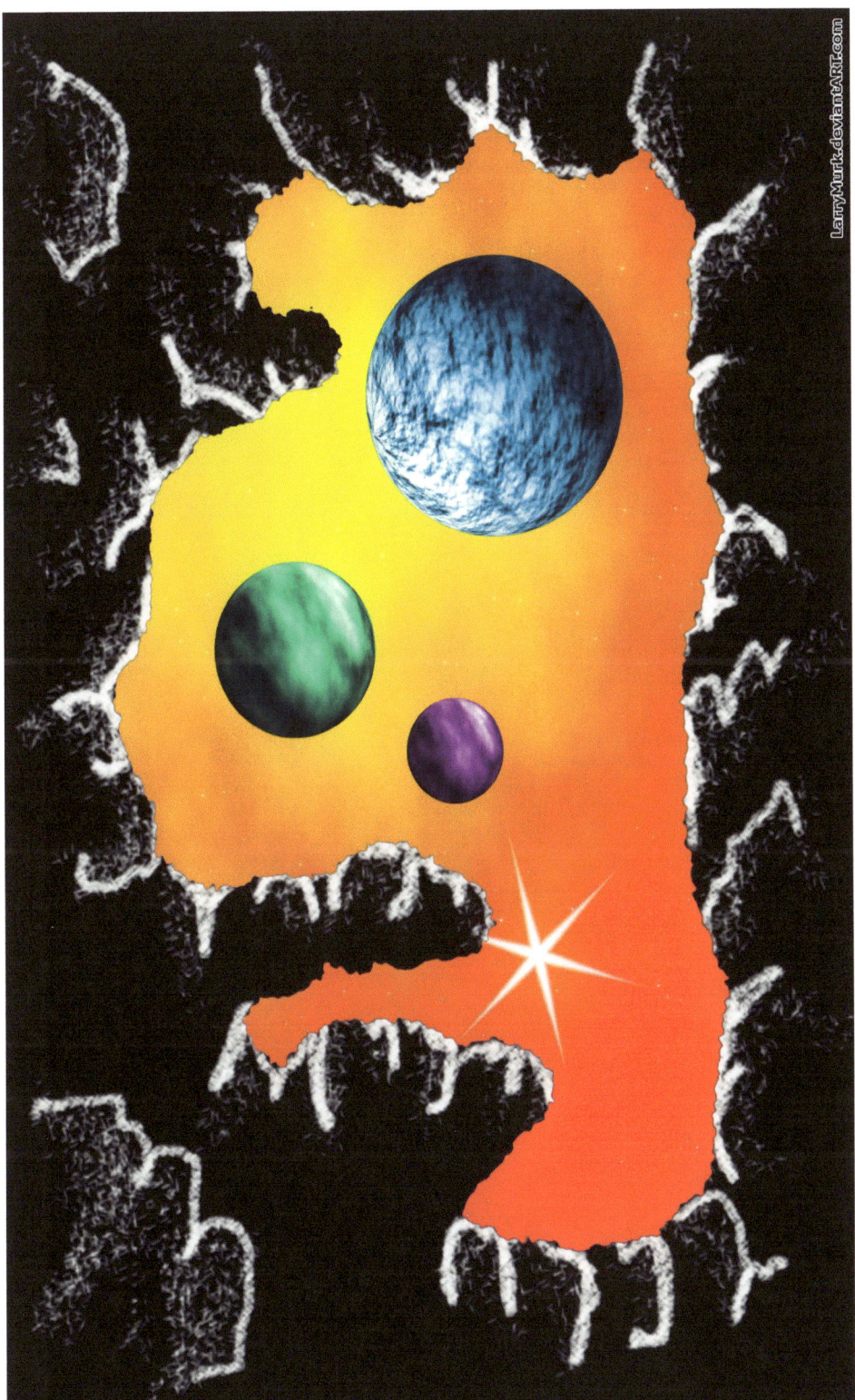

Cityscape with Bright Sky

City lights etch their image across the night time's dark canvas only to be outdone by the sky's fantastic purple illuminating rays.

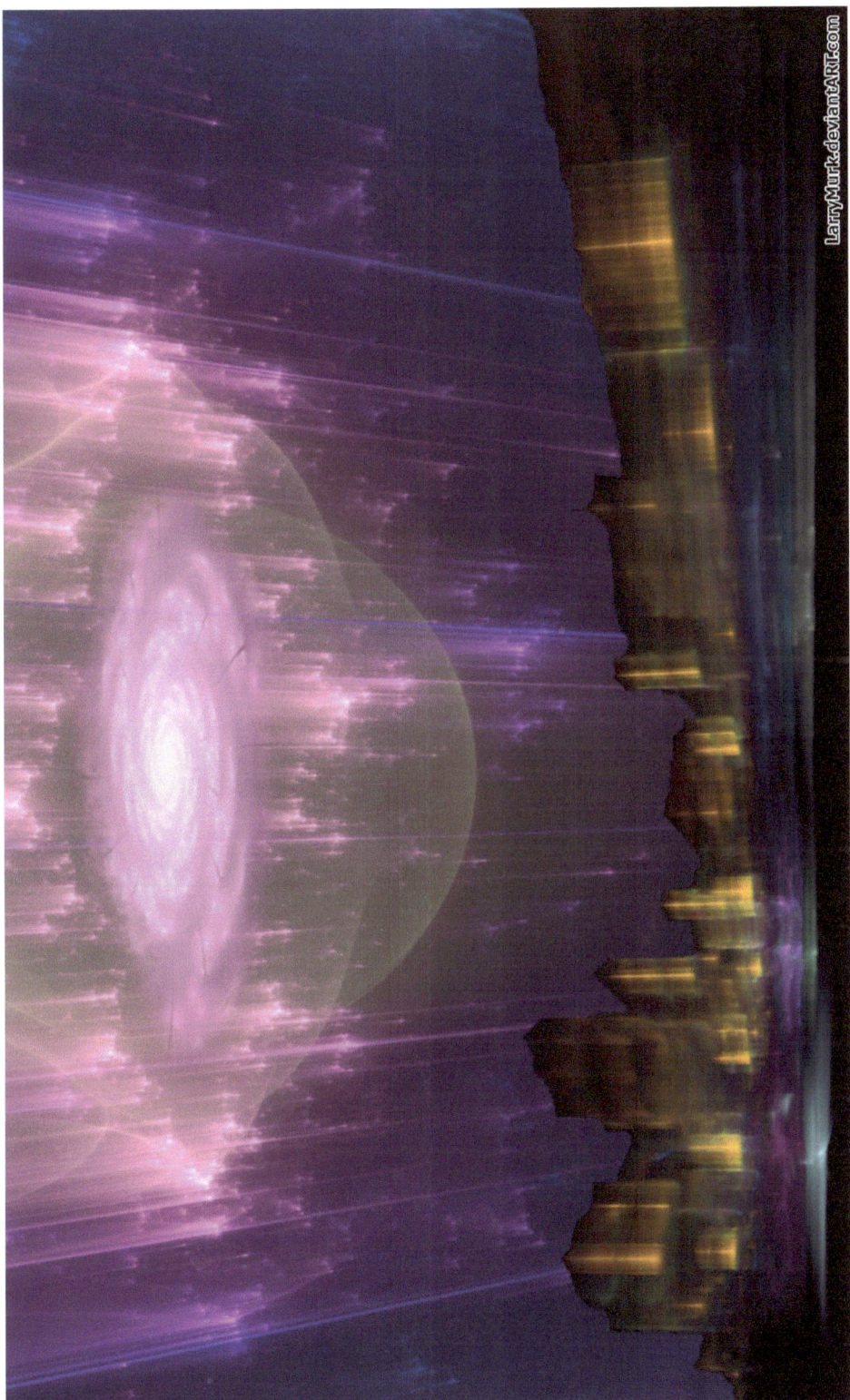

Snow Covered Tree

Snow blankets a lonely tree creating a most picturesque sight to behold.

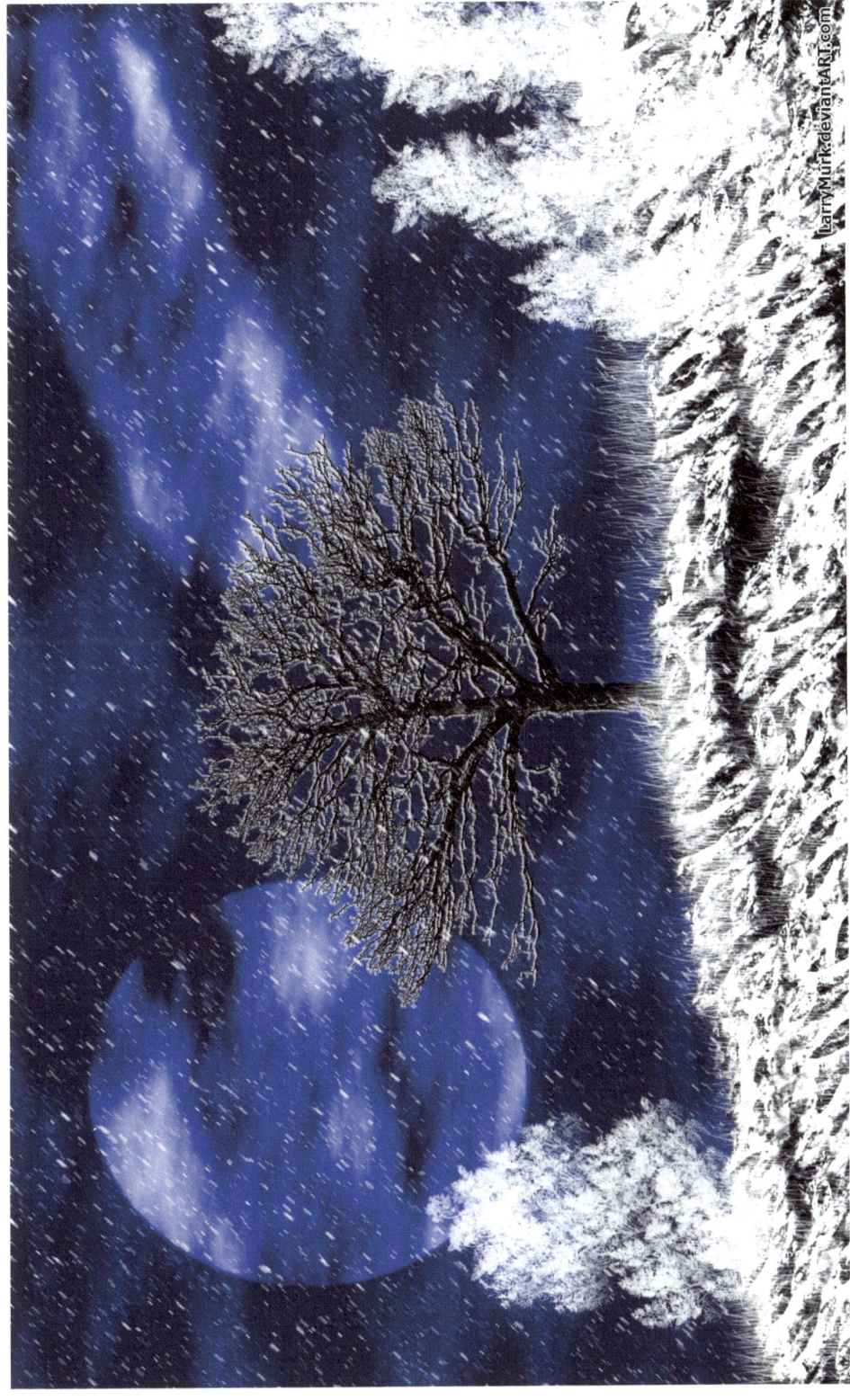